Robert S Bowden 1995

UNIVERSE

Manhattan in Detail

*An Intimate Portrait
in Watercolor*

ROBERT L. BOWDEN

MANHATTAN
IN
DETAIL

*An
Intimate
Portrait
in
Watercolor*

ROBERT L. BOWDEN

UNIVERSE

East 82nd Street between First and Second Avenues of historic Yorkville is only a few blocks away from Brandy's Piano Bar, a local favorite dating back to the speakeasy 1920s. Nearby Carl Schurz Park houses Gracie Mansion, the official residence of the mayor of New York City.

Acknowledgments
My thanks to my daughter Lisa Carter and her husband Warren who first encouraged me to paint on the streets of Manhattan; to my publisher Charles Miers who has made this book possible; my editor Jessica Fuller for her patience and guidance once again; for the concise descriptions by Monique Peterson of my subjects; for the computer skills of Matt Hildebrand in design production and most of all for Diana, who continues to constantly support and encourage my ideas and efforts.

First published in the United States of America in 2008
by UNIVERSE PUBLISHING
A Division of Rizzoli International Publications, Inc.
300 Park Avenue South
New York, NY 10010
www.rizzoliusa.com

© 2008 Robert L. Bowden

2008 2009 2010 2011 2012 / 10 9 8 7 6 5 4 3 2 1

Design by Robert L. Bowden
Printed in China

ISBN 10: 0-7893-1691-9
ISBN 13: 978-0-7893-1691-2
Library of Congress Catalog Control Number: 2007938619

FRONT END PAPER:
Reservoir at E. 90th St. looking west. 1995.
HALF TITLE PAGE:
Morgan Library, E. 37th St. towards Empire State Building. 1995.
TITLE PAGE:
E. 82nd St. and Fifth Ave. opposite the Metropolitan Museum of Art. 1995.
OPPOSITE:
4. E. 82nd St. between First and Second Aves. 1996.

St. Luke's Place is a quaint two-block stretch between Hudson and Bleecker Streets in the West Village. The Renaissance Revival style buildings along St. Luke's once housed playboy mayor of New York, "Beau" James Walker, poet Marianne Moore, painter Paul Cadmus, and author Theodore Dreiser.

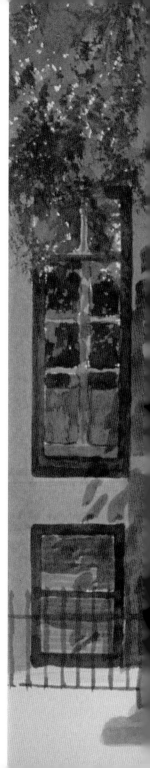

5. *St. Luke's Place, Greenwich Village.* 1995.

2007 [signature]

The celebrated Prometheus fountain at Rockefeller Center is the iconic figure overlooking the skating rink in Rockefeller Center's sunken plaza. The eight-ton bronze-gilded statue celebrating the Greek legend of Titan was brought to life by early twentieth-century American sculptor Paul Howard Manship in 1934.

6. *Prometheus at Rockefeller Center.* 2007.

The intersection of East 92nd Street and Madison Avenue lies in the heart of Carnegie Hill. Residents consider the Upper East Side between 86th and 94th Streets one of New York's best-kept secrets. The community is an eclectic architectural blend of brownstones, townhouses, mansions, wood-built homes, and pre-war apartments.

7. *East 92nd Street and Madison Avenue.* 1996.

ONE WAY

ONE WAY

WALK

CATERING
GIFT BASKETS
WE DELIVER

Canard and Company

GIFT BASK

Originally conceived as the Museum of Non-Objective Painting, the Solomon R. Guggenheim Foundation's collection of significant modern works opened in 1939. Twenty years and more than 700 drawings later, Frank Lloyd Wright's architectural experience offers visitors a unique and eloquent presentation of design and art.

8. *Solomon R. Guggenheim Museum.* 1995.

THE THANNHAUSE...

THE ...MUSE

Robert G. Bouwen 1905

Open to the public on October 27, 1904, the Astor Place
subway entrance, designed by Heins & LaFarge, lies in
the heart of Greenwich Village at the junction of Bowery,
Astor Place, and Lafayette Street. The beaver motifs in the
architecture are a nod to business mogul John Jacob Astor's
involvement in the fur trade.

9. *Entrance to Subway at Astor Place.* 1995.

Robert F. Bowden 1995

The intersection of Broadway and West 42nd Street celebrated for its massive signage, neon lights, and theaters is one of the most populous locales in the entire city. Times Square acquired its name on April 8, 1904, when publisher Adolph S. Ochs moved *The New York Times* to the area.

OPPOSITE
The bend in the road on Commerce Street where it meets Barrow is a delightful section of the West Village with reminders of its pastoral history. The Cherry Lane Theater, founded by Edna St. Vincent Millay, was once a farm silo. Nearby, Chumley's, a still-operating speakeasy, was a former blacksmith's shop.

PRECEDING SPREAD
10. *Times Square, from Broadway and W. 42nd St.* 2007.

OPPOSITE
11. *Love Machine at Commerce and Barrow Sts., West Village.* 2007.

Robert F. Bowden 2007

The 42-foot *Group of Four Trees* sculpture by Jean Dubuffet graces the modern steel-framed rectangular skyscraper that serves as the headquarters of Chase Manhattan Bank. Designed by architect Gordon Bunshaft, the aluminum and glass surfaces of the 60-floor, 813-foot building offer a commanding presence with all its light-reflecting surfaces.

12. *Chase Manhattan Plaza.* 1995.

Robert Bowden 1995

Robert Bowden 1995

PRECEDING SPREAD

A favored gathering place of NYU students and avid chess players, Greenwich Village's Washington Square Park started out as an eight-acre parcel purchased by the city to function as a potter's field and public gallows. Its signature arch designed by Stanford White celebrates George Washington's presidential inauguration.

OPPOSITE

The charming Italian bakery in the heart of Soho on Prince Street between Broadway and Thompson has a long-standing tradition in the community. Anthony Dapolito, known and loved as the unofficial mayor of Greenwich Village established the bakery and named it after a volcano in Italy near his family's home.

PRECEDING SPREAD
13. *Washington Square, Greenwich Village.* 1995.

OPPOSITE
14. *Vesuvio Bakery, Soho.* 2007.

Robert F. Bowden 2007

23

OPPOSITE
The birth of the world's leading stock exchange took place in May, 1792 underneath a Buttonwood tree outside 68 Wall Street. There, twenty-four merchants and stockbrokers signed an agreement to trade securities. Then, five securities trades. Today, the New York Stock Exchange trades more than 1.46 billion shares of stock.

BELOW
After the 1987 stock market crash, Arturo Di Modica sculpted the seven-thousand pound *Charging Bull* and installed the uncommissioned art in front of the New York Stock Exchange. The police impounded the beast, but public outcry forced the city to find a permanent home for the sculpture at Bowling Green.

Opposite
15. *New York Stock Exchange.* 1995.

Below
16. *The Bull Sculpture at Bowling Green,* 2007.

Park Avenue and East 79th Street is part of the northern boundary of the Lenox Hill neighborhood on the Upper East Side. The community was born from the land of real estate mogul Robert Lenox, whose 300-acre farm once graced the area.

17. *Park Ave. and E. 79th St.* 1996.

PARK

Designed by John A. Roebling and Wilhelm Hildenbrand, the
Brooklyn Bridge is one of the oldest suspension bridges in the
United States. The bridge was the first to employ pneumatic caisson
engineering, giving the bridge's piers better stability underwater.
Roebling declared, "As a great work of art, and a successful
specimen of advanced bridge engineering, the structure will forever
testify to the energy, enterprise, and wealth of that community."

Emma Stebbins was the first woman to receive a commission for a
major work of public art in New York City. Her gift: the *Angel of the
Waters*, which adorns Central Park's Bethesda Fountain. The iconic
figure symbolizes the first fresh water to arrive in a plague-ridden
New York.

Preceding Spread
18. *The Brooklyn Bridge.* 1999.

Opposite
19. *Bethesda Fountain, Central Park.* 1995.

Robert Bowden 1995

Business tycoon Frank W. Woolworth purchased the lot at the northeast corner of 80th and Fifth Avenue and commissioned architect C. P. H. Gilbert, known for his signature French Renaissance style, to build his home as well as the adjacent three houses for his daughters, including Number 2, East 80th Street.

20. *Number 2, E. 80th St.* 1995.

The corner of Lexington Avenue and East 92nd Street has been a long-standing corner for neighborhood restaurants, including the former venues of La Collina, Café Lex, and Lex 92. The area is home to one of the city's favored cultural arts centers, The 92nd Street Y.

21. *Restaurant Set-up with Taxi.* 1996.

West 57th Street has prestigious roots as home to some of New York's wealthiest families including the Roosevelts and Juilliards. Randolph Almiroty designed the reconstruction of the brownstone at No. 31 adding a triple-vaulted interior ceiling to the landmark building that now houses the Rizzoli Bookstore.

22. Rizzoli Bookstore, W. 57th St. 2007.

RIZZOLI

RIZZOLI

Robert Bowden 2007

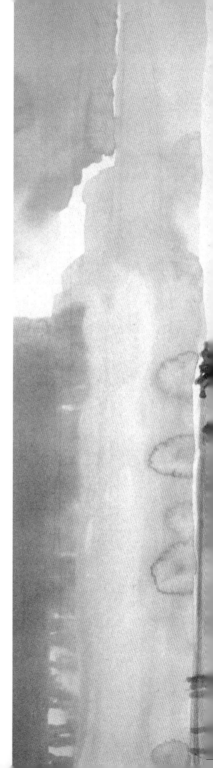

PRECEDING SPREAD
The Metropolitan Museum of Art, designed
by architectural masters Calvert Vaux and
Jacob Wrey Mold, is among the world's
largest fine art collections. Each year more
than five million people visit the museum's
vast holdings of more than 6,500 pieces of art
displayed over some two million square feet.

OPPOSITE
Built in the 1880s, The Dakota apartments
on 72nd Street are so-called for being as
remote as the Dakota Territory at the time
of its construction. The legendary building
has been home to John Lennon, Boris
Karloff, Judy Garland, and Mia Farrow's
fictional character in the chilling horror,
Rosemary's Baby.

PRECEDING SPREAD
23. *The Metropolitan Museum of Art.* 1995.

OPPOSITE
24. *The Dakota.* 1995.

The New York Public Library, designed by architects Carrère and Hastings, is renowned for its impressive reading room and collections stored along more than 75 miles of shelves. The guardian lions Patience and Fortitude greet patrons as they enter.

Jacqueline Kennedy Onassis' passionate dedication to the preservation and restoration of one of New York's most beloved landmarks is in large part the reason why Grand Central Station still stands today. The terminal is a daily crossroads for millions, viewed here through the windows of the Sony Building.

25. *The New York Public Library.* 2007.

26. *Grand Central Station seen from inside Sony Bldg.* 1995.

The John Finley Walk makes up the picturesque stretch of the East River Esplanade between 80th and 90th Streets. The oldest portion of Manhattan's Waterfront Greenway, it offers unobstructed views of Randall's Island, the Triborough Bridge, Hell Gate Bridge, Queens and Brooklyn.

27. *The John Finley Walk, Yorkville.* 1996.

Robert L Bowden October 1996

The tree-lined streets of the Upper East Side offer some of New York's most elegant and luxurious neighborhoods, shops, and cultural institutions. The corner of Madison Avenue and East 93rd Street includes a collection of New American and French bistros, including Demi at 1316 Madison.

28. Number 81 E. 93rd St. and Demi at E. 93rd St. and Madison Ave. 1995.

81 E. 73rd St and DEMI at 93rd & Madison Ave.

The architectural team of Heins & LaFarge designed the brick and stone control house that shelters the subway entrance at West 72nd Street between Broadway and Amsterdam. Completely renovated in 2002, the historical landmark is only one of three remaining control houses in all of New York City.

29. *W. 72nd St. Control House, Broadway and Amsterdam Ave.* 1995.

A contender in New York's skyscraper race, the Art Deco Chrysler building with its 60-foot steel spire, became the world's tallest building in 1930. Architect William Van Alen pays tribute to Chrysler with automobile themes evident throughout. Look for radiator caps and ornamental car wheels.

30. *Chrysler Building from Lexington Ave. and E. 36th St.* 2007.

Robert S. Borden 10/96

This four-star restaurant, favored by literati, celebrities, politicians, and VIPs has been a New York City hot spot for decades. Immortalized in Woody Allen's *Manhattan*. The Upper East-side establishment is still a standard for A-listers. Elaine herself makes regular appearances to welcome her patrons.

OPPOSITE
Designed by architect Emery Roth in the 1920s, the San Remo apartment building, as seen here from Central Park, was the first of its kind with its twin-tower model. Roth modeled the tower's circular temples after the Greek Choragic Monument of Lysicrates.

PRECEDING SPREAD
31. *Elaine's*. 1996.

OPPOSITE
32. *The San Remo from Central Park*. 1995.

Robert J. Bowden 1975

PRECEDING SPREAD
The Cooper Union for the Advancement of Science and Art is the only full-scholarship establishment of higher learning dedicated to architecture and engineering. It's the legacy of Peter Cooper, an entrepreneur of humble beginnings who designed the nation's first steam engine. Thomas Edison is one of the school's esteemed students.

OPPOSITE
The rowhouses along 73rd Street between Central Park West and Columbus Avenue are among the first residential projects to punctuate the wild open countryside and vast farmland that now makes up the Upper West Side. Dakota architect Henry J. Hardenbergh designed these with an eye toward distinction, variety, and harmony.

PRECEDING SPREAD
33. *Cooper Union.* 1996.

OPPOSITE
34. *W. 73rd St. between Central Park West and Columbus Ave.* 1995.

A popular sunbathing and picnicking spot in the warm months, Bryant Park offers free concerts, entertainment, and outdoor movies. It is also the city's first wireless park, a testament to its numerous laptop wielding patrons.

Architect Daniel Burnham designed New York City's first skyscraper at the intersection of 23rd Street, Broadway, and Fifth Avenue. It is a combination of Gothic and Renaissance styles. Critics of the 22-story Flatiron Building feared the structure would not stay erect, and nicknamed it "Burnham's Folly."

35. *Bryant Park.* 2007.

36. *The Flatiron Building.* 1995.

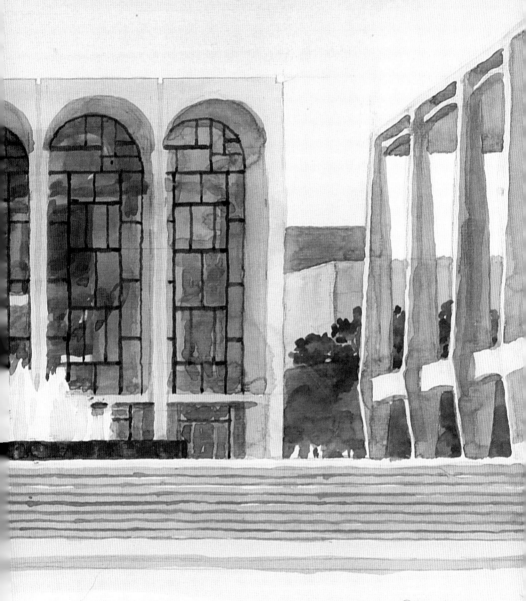

Robert L Bowden 2007

PRECEDING SPREAD
The Lincoln Center Urban Renewal Project began in 1955, with the New York Philharmonic, the Metropolitan Opera, and The Julliard School among its first constituents. John D. Rockefeller III served as president of the Lincoln Center for Performing Arts, a collection of buildings that served dance, theater, and music.

OPPOSITE
The red brick and brownstone Renaissance Revival structure at 34 Gramercy Park is the oldest cooperative apartment house in Manhattan. Designed by architect George DaCunha, realtors billed the 48-unit building as French Flats, to distinguish it from ordinary tenements. All residents receive a key to the gated private park.

PRECEDING SPREAD
37. *Lincoln Center.* 2007.

OPPOSITE
38. *34 Gramercy Park.* 1995.

Robert F Barden / 2007

The stretch of landmark townhouses along East 137th Street
in Harlem Heights is known as Strivers' Row. Stanford White
designed the Italianate structures, which quickly became home
to the aristocratic residents of the area. They are some of the
few blocks in the city with an alleyway.

Completed in 1909, the Queensboro Bridge designed by
Gustav Lindenthal opened the doors to the development of
Queens. The cantilever bridge, which crosses over Randall's
Island, is one of seven that spans the sixteen-mile tidal straight
known as New York's East River.

39. *Strivers' Row, E. 137th St., Harlem Heights.* 2007.

40. *East River near E. 70th St.* 1996.

Robert Bowden 2007

PRECEDING SPREAD
An annex of the Metropolitan Museum of art lies nestled among the wooded cliffs of Fort Tyron Park. The Cloisters house the museum's collection of medieval architecture and art, notably the rare tapestries and magnificently illustrated Book of Hours. The area was inhabited by the Wickquasgeck Tribe until the 1600s.

OPPOSITE
The spires of New York City's oldest Roman Catholic church rise 330 feet from street level. Architect James Renwick, designer of Grace Church, the Smithsonian, and the New York Public Library masterminded St. Patrick's Cathedral as a Gothic-influenced structure, distinctive in its style and harmonious proportions.

PRECEDING SPREAD
41. *The Cloisters.* 2007.

OPPOSITE
42. *St. Patrick's Cathedral.* 2007.

Robert S. Bowden

List of Watercolors

1. *Reservoir at E. 90th St., looking west.* 1995. 7 ¹⁄₁₆" x 14 ¾", (detail)* Front end paper
2. *Morgan Library, E. 37th St. towards Empire State Building.* 1995. 11 ¼" x 9 ⅜" * Half title page
3. *E. 82nd St. and Fifth Ave. opposite the Metropolitan Museum of Art.* 1995. 13 ¾ x 7 ⅛ *Title page
4. *E. 82nd St. between First and Second Aves.* 1996. 12" x 7 ½" * page 3
5. *St. Luke's Place, Greenwich Village.* 1995. 9 ⅛" x 8 ½" * pages 4/5
6. *Prometheus at Rockefeller Center.* 2007. 10" x 10" ** pages 6/7
7. *E. 92nd St. and Madison Ave.* 1996. 16" x 14" * pages 8/9
8. *Solomon R. Guggenheim Museum.* 1995. 14" x 11 ½" * page 11
9. *Entrance to Subway at Astor Place.* 1995. 6" x 10 ½" * pages 12/13
10. *Times Square from Broadway and W. 42nd St.* 2007. 13 ½" x 18 ½" ** pages 14/15
11. *Love Machine at Commerce and Barrow Sts., West Village.* 2007. 18 ½ x 13 ½, (detail)** page 17
12. *Chase Manhattan Plaza.* 1995. 10 ⅛" x 4 ¹³⁄₁₆" (detail) ** page 19
13. *Washington Square, Greenwich Village.* 1995. 9 ¹¹⁄₁₆" x 12" * pages 20/21
14. *Vesuvio Bakery, So Ho.* 2007. 10" x 6 ½" ** page 23
15. *New York Stock Exchange.* 1995. 13 ³⁄₁₆" x 10 ½" * pages 24/25
16. *The Bull Sculpture at Bowling Green.* 2007. 6" x 6" ** page 24
17. *Park Ave. and E. 79th St.* 1996. 17 ½" x 9 ¼" ** page 27
18. *The Brooklyn Bridge.* 1999. 17 ½" x 23", (detail)* pages 28/29
19. *Bethesda Fountain, Central Park.* 1995. 13 ¼" x 8 ½"* page 31
20. *Number 2, E .80th St.* 1995. 12 ⅜ x 7 ⅜"* page 33
21. *Restaurant Set-up with Taxi.* 1996. 10" x 9"* pages 34/35
22. *Rizzoli Bookstore, W. 57th St.* 2007. 18 ½" x 13 ½" ** page 37
23. *The Metropolitan Museum of Art.* 1995. 13 ³⁄₁₆ x 16 ⁵⁄₁₆ * pages 38/39 (also on jacket front cover)
24. *The Dakota.* 1995. 15 ⅝" x 14 ⅞" * pages 40/41
25. *The New York Public Library.* 2007. 13 ½" x 18 ½" ** pages 42/43
26. *Grand Central Station seen from inside the Sony Building.* 1995. 14 ⅛" x 7 ¹⁵⁄₁₆" * page 45
27. *John Finley Walk, Yorkville.* 1996. 11" x 14" ** pages 46/47
28. *Number 81 E. 93rd St. and Demi at E. 93rd. St. and Madison Ave.* 1995. 15 ⅜ x 10 ⅝ * page 49
29. *W. 72nd St. Control House, Broadway at Amsterdam Ave.* 1995. 8 ⅞"x 10 ⅝" * pages 50/51
30. *Chrysler Building from Lexington Ave. and E. 36th St.* 2007. 18 ½"x 13 ½" ** page 52
31. *Elaine's.* 1996. 11" x 14" * pages 54/55
32. *The San Remo from Central Park.* 1995. 11 ⅝" x 10" * page 57
33. *Cooper Union.* 1996. 13 ¼" x 19" ** pages 58/59
34. *W. 73rd St. between Central Park West and Columbus Ave.* 1995. 14 ³⁄₁₆ x 8 ¹¹⁄₁₆ * page 61
35. *Bryant Park.* 2007. 13 ½" x 18 ½" ** pages 62/63
36. *The Flatiron Building.* 1995. 15 ⅛" x 8 ⅜" * page 65
37. *Lincoln Center.* 2007. 13 ½" x 18 ½" ** pages 66/67
38. *34 Gramercy Park.* 1995. 5 ¹⁵⁄₁₆" x 4 ¹⁵⁄₁₆" * page 69
39. *Strivers' Row, W. 137th St., Harlem Heights.* 2007. 13 ½" x 18 ½" ** pages 70/71
40. *East River near E. 70th St.* 1996. 12" x 12" * page 73
41. *The Cloisters.* 2007. 13 ½" x 18 ½" * pages 74/75
42. *St. Patrick's Cathedral.* 2007. 18 ½" x 13 ½" page 77
43. *Statue of Liberty from Ellis Island.* 1999. 12" x 18" * end paper, end of book
44. *Row of Four on Second Ave. at E. 82nd St.* 1996. 12" x 18" ** jacket, back cover

* Private collection
** Artist's collection

43. Following Spread, Back end paper: *Statue of Liberty from Ellis Island.* 1999.

44. Jacket Back Cover: *Row of Four on Second Ave. at E. 82nd St.* 1996.